Rush Hour Flowers

A Collection of Poems

Tracy Monaco

ISBN 978-1-365-88211-1

for my brother George

Marble Playground

The sun falls
from the toxic sky,
we laugh, while it dies,
and time chips away,
at marble hearts
while we play above
what we will become…

Decrepit flowers
crumbling in the breeze,
whispering from the trees,
keep on searching
for what we used to be,
the shadows fall
and we see through our perfect
slumber
-1990

The Dark Years

There's not a day that goes by,
that she doesn't think about the day
that goes by,
that she doesn't think about
the day…
7AM- Treatment time again,
mouth dry
needle in arm
mask over face
the white blurs take their place,
time to clear away the cobwebs
Struggling, she
falls
from their world of
light
and floats
into her familiar shadows
below…

In the distance
she hears their voices
she cannot move a single muscle,
not wanting to return,
she continues
to float
in anesthetic bliss…

For years, she'd been dying,
smothered in the cobwebs
thoughts of suicide
trapped in her mind
seventeen years wide
She prayed for dissolution

They wheel her down the hall,
back behind locked doors
where they think she belongs,
where they think she belongs

7AM-Treatment time again,
mouth dry
needle in arm
mask over face
The white blurs take their place,
with their special blend
electric fire,
it's time to clear away the cobwebs,
please
clear away the cobwebs,
she has to live.

There's not a day that goes by,
That she doesn't think about the day
That goes by,
That she doesn't think about
The day…
her sanity began to creep away.
-1994

Shadows slowly drift
in the early morning night,
Laughter spreads cool
through the sweet haze
of our small room gliding
in-between the space
between spaces hiding

Lush realities flow
beneath tepid moonlight,
Answers behind
whispers lure us
towards the ocean's ledge,
rediscovering
soft life pushed to the edge.

Eastern twilight swears to
consume the bright smiles
rusted to our faces

oh so tired with thought too deep,
in-between the spaces
where time never sleeps.

-1994

Beltway Life

Metal beasts
crawl behind
the graveled wall
outside my bedroom window.

Their anger
endlessly
hums
through the thin glass,
through the taped cracks

Old woman house-
Her slanted beauty
shudders and groans
with each passing sound

Her memories layered in

dust and smog
Created by
the metal beasts that
impatiently
surrounds us all.

-1996

Bouncin' down the road
in my rusty ol' pick-up truck,
Good music pierces the surrounding scene,
A red crescent moon hangs low
in her cool October evening,
The liquor store's warm neon wine,
Barbed wire fences
scar the dim reflective sky.

Can't wait to smell the next day's
Fall colors,
-then came that familiar curve
and those headlights hit me
so fast and hard…

Throwing me into a river of darkness
Sweeping me out to sea
Swimming through the lonely shadows,
Floating amid the debris,

Hearing the echoes of autumn,
The lighthouse beckoning me

-10/1996

Watch the day
take its nap among the stars,
Like hugging an old friend goodbye,
it's warmth can be felt
by the mere thought
of the way it makes you feel
when near by

Close your eyes-
Taste the ocean song-
Hear the summer breeze,
dance with the leaves
Is why I want to breathe

-1998

Kite in the sky
I'm faded from the sun
Take many dives
still not broken
Tattered wings
still I fly strong
Cast my shadow on the soft sand below
Trail across the indigo sky
closer to the smile above

The string snaps!
and I am on my own...
until I spiral into the hard sea

I wish I had enjoyed the view more,
but what did I know,
I was just a kite
struggling to be free.
-1999

Together
we watch the winter lake-
with passionate vision
through delicate mist
we dream...

Raw beneath the summer,
sweet music drips down her back,
I swim to her ship
and whisper
I love you.

-2000

You will see
a lot of people
creepin' through and breakin' backs
against the rocks
we stood upon
to be tall
Sifting time
through paper towel filters,
The human sand
tight as asphalt,
Hugging roads
blanketed by salt, hurriedly melting
in time for
rush hour flowers
caked
in 24 hour convenience searchlights-
Bleaching our vision of spirit,
Blinding us to rescue.
-2001

Under warm pink clouds
You were born.
Sailing upon life's delicate fabric,
The water weaves your presence-
Your light brightens our world.
May God's gentle winds
Fill your heart always...

-2003

Wrapped in the darkness of her night
Her skin smooth as moonlight
Shadows of snowflakes
Sparkle like her kisses
Her fingers stroke my curly tresses

Put your hand on my scared chest
Feel your warm wind
Steal my breath
You touch my heart
You touch my heart

Falling in the brightness of her stars
Her eyes I swim in from afar,
Her sun speaks
like sweet whispers
slips her arms around me
I listen

Put your hand on my soft face,
Your warm wind
I must chase
All I have to give is love,
You touch my heart
You touch my heart

-2003

The mountain's silhouette-
Her shadow.
The wide dirt trail quieted by time,
a relic of the railroad
that once traveled through,
now crunching contently
beneath my boots.

A small lemon flies by,
while the crisp air
invigorates my thoughts-
The smell of pine touches something
elusive and ancient
deep inside my chest-
And still the grey clouds
incessantly hide Her blue skies
that I long to see...

Waiting for a ray of sunshine

to warm my pale face,
Gazing out at the valley below,
comforts my soul,
helping me
walk closer with God.

-2003

Wandering upon
shards of glass
cutting my bare heart
chasing these ashes

With all these possibilities
I cannot grasp
like sand in my hair
I have no choice
but to brush them out,
they go quickly
down the drain
my soul goes too
into that dark place

Would you go there with me?
Would you fish me out?
Hook me-
make me your catch?

Where are you?

-2003

Staring out at the horizon
waiting... wanting...

Your sun burnt my cheek,
Your sand abrased my passion-

Lost my edge
Took a tumble
in shallow water
Tossed around
There is no air

Ghost crabs safe from the sea,
Honest jellyfish respectfully sting me,
Paddling out here alone-
this current I cannot fight
So we all must go...

Lost my edge

Took a tumble
In shallow water
Tossed around
There is no air

My breath,
I surrender
This butterfly
Floats on

-2003

God, please take this from me
Take this cement necklace
These sour thoughts
Please help me

This shadow over the Earth
casts doubt upon me,
searching... searching...

My head
floats back and forth
like a leaf on a breeze,
Broken view,
I cannot rest

Tired of these extremes
stretching my mind,
Hate these strobing images
filling my teeth

singeing my bones
Want to sleep
Take this mediocrity
Take this anxiety

When will you rinse off this sadness,
in time for the sunrise?
Please bless me
Sprinkle my thirsty face
Don't waste it watering asphalt
Cool this sickness off

Can hardly move this shell,
I want to run away
but there's no where to go anyway,
So I get these words out... out... out...
I expel you!
SHREDDED
EXHAUSTED
DEVESTATED

BLENDED
WOVEN
in the blackness bleeding
down my brick wall
Crawling over these damp fears,
I want to disappear,
Am I always to feel like an imposter.
-2003

For some reason,
I've grown fond of the cold,
embraced the darkness,
taken refuge in the shadows

Its stillness calms my mind
Yet I cannot find comfort in any season
Seems there is always a wind
that dilutes my soul
which makes me ache for
something beyond my grasp

But like a rock,
my heart is strong,
pain chips away at it,
but refuses bitterness,
Fragmented in my emotional betrayal,
I deceive myself.

My presence isn't strong
but my integrity is true,
My shoes are shiny,
haven't I proved my worthiness?
When will I be good enough?

I'm like a piece of paper
blowing down the black street,
Don't know where I am or
where I'm going,
Waiting for breadcrumbs...
Will I always be disappointed.
-2003

To the sun I go
Spinning my light
No more running from life
Still there is pain
Fields of flowers
dried and burnt
But at least the sky is blue
And the air is warm
Tender thoughts water my roots
From this winter I must wake
To the sun I go

-2004

Through the mist, your lighthouse
shines like the sun-

Floating in your cool dark ocean
the tide pulls me closer to your shore,
Underneath the gentle waves
I hold my breath-
And emerge to feel your warm breeze
against my face-

Towards your light...
I swim.

-2004

Insomnia

Exhaustion scratches at me
My dreams static on the TV
Lost on this raft
Floating on this sleepless sea
Life piling in the corner
with the old, crunchy leaves

-2004

I sit
alone

cold Colorado rain
blesses my bare skin

thunder vibrates through me,
delicate yellow flowers
stand with courage
as the storm begins

Hummingbirds unseen
shrill between the gusts of wind and
I find myself wishing
the little birds would take shelter
in the hollow of my heart
and make me whole again

It's quiet now-

A sliver of blue
looks down upon me,
The storm pressing through-
Breathing God deeply

I stand
With renewed Faith.
-2004

I don’t sleep-
but I dream
about holding you.
Your clear blue eyes
quench my thirst,
Your words
feed my hunger.

My heart opens and closes
like the moon rising and falling,
In my dreams
your glance pries my heart open-
For a brief moment
I smile-
I am close to you.

I want to dance with you –
slow- in the candle light,
passionate kisses to sooth my soul,

I wouldn't mind
hiding in your depths
tasting your essence
drowning in your affection.

Watching the sunset and the sunrise-
Counting stars through the slow air,
Crying through the lost nights,
Thoughts of you gently comfort me
So I dove into your laughter,
dropped anchor in your harbor,
Can I swim in your music forever?

What I would trade for a sip of you
-200?

The Carnivore

Devouring me
with your words
Your appetite
is never satisfied
The hole never filled
What is gained
By me you drain

You feed on my shadow
Tearing at my fabric
Frozen in the winter of your madness
I can hardly move

Why did I stay?

-2004

Back in the Day

West of Denver
through the tunnel
lies the mountains
of my heart

Top of the world
Rocky Mountain, mine forever-
seize the day

Flying down that mountain of snow
Carving tracks through pine trees below
Bright blue skies
quiet so slow

East of Denver
far away there is the ocean
of my mind

Hurricane
You should've been here yesterday
chargin' waves

Gliding down that mountain of glass
Catching waves like it's your last
Bright blue skies
now it has passed

North of Denver
West of Boulder
lies the mountains
of my soul

Top of the world
Looking out at forever
powder dreams

Sliding down that mountain of snow

Catchin' air –Eddie would go
Bright blue skies
white wind blows

Heart mind and soul
We prayed for snow
back in the day

Heart mind and soul
We prayed for waves
back in the day

We prayed for snow
We prayed for waves
Back in the day

We prayed for snow
We prayed for waves
Back in the day

Back in the day
Heart mind and soul
Back in the day

-200?

Rush Hour Flowers is a collection of poems written by Tracy Monaco in the 1990's and early 2000's. She has a Bachelor of Arts from the University of Maryland and two "Editor's Choice Awards for Outstanding Achievement in Poetry" from the National Library of Poetry. She is also a musician, composer, songwriter, recording artist, and photographer. You can find out more about her at: www.NeptunesDaughter.com

www.ingramcontent.com/pod-product-compliance
Ingram Content Group UK Ltd.
Pitfield, Milton Keynes, MK11 3LW, UK
UKHW020216250726
13967UKWH00001B/18

9 781365 882111